This book is ded

C000099213

Allan Si......
(1929-94)

Northumbrian Scribe

Be present, O merciful God, and protect
us through the silent hours of this
night, so that we who are wearied
by the changes and chances
of this fleeting world, may repose
upon thy eternal changelessness,
through Jesus Christ our Lord. Amen.

From the Service of Compline

FROM A
DRAWING
BY ALLAN
SMALE

CONTENTS

*The symbols for the 4 Evangelists
are based on those in the Book of Kells
preserved in Trinity College Dublin:
St. Matthew (a bull);
St. Mark (a lion);
St. Luke (an angel);
and St. John (an eagle).*

INTRODUCTION

In the half-light of a cold winter's afternoon at Escomb, I talked with Norma Smale who was visiting the ancient Saxon Church shortly after the death of her husband Allan. He had been a member of the Northumbrian Scribes, a group of calligraphers formed in 1988 and who are now tutored by Susan Moor. I had recently returned from Holy Island where I had reflected on the texts in the Library of Marygate House, produced by another group of Scribes brought together by the Chaplaincy to the Arts and Recreation in the North East. Norma Smale and I dreamed of turning the church at Escomb into a Scriptorium and of inviting the Scribes to use Escomb as their inspiration for a collection of texts which might appeal to a wider readership. This book is the product of that vision.

The tradition of writing illustrated manuscripts in the monasteries of Northumberland and Durham died out with the invention of printing at the end of the fifteenth century. The faith and craftsmanship which inspired such work can still be seen in the survival of the Lindisfarne Gospels in the British Library, the Codex Amiatinus in Florence and in a number of important manuscripts preserved in Durham Cathedral. This tradition is now being resurrected in Northumbria and throughout Britain by groups of enthusiasts seeking to enter and build upon this foundation. In China it has always been recognised that pictographic writing is an art form of great beauty and spiritual significance, and we in the West are now rediscovering the power and potential of the word made personal.

This book is rooted in the intermingling of Celtic and Saxon cultures that make up the Northumbrian tradition. The ancient church at Escomb, built at the end of the seventh century, is a living witness to the world of Aidan, Bede and Cuthbert. The Northumberland Scribes have used texts of their own choice and some selected by the congregation at Escomb. Here you will find prayers, Biblical texts and themes which have come to have personal significance in a particular place, but which may also give inspiration and joy to those with eyes to see.

Nicholas Beddow – Vicar of Escomb

R McManners 96

scomb is on the road to nowhere. People who come to visit the church have first to find the way. Some make the journey because they are experts in church architecture, or are brought as students of Archaeology or Early English History. School children are guided round the church and tourists use their leaflets and guide books. Others are drawn off the busy A68 on route to Hadrian's Wall or when returning from a holiday in Scotland. Some visitors see only the past and are disappointed by the Council housing and the modern setting, but others grasp that here is a place that speaks of a living continuity of faith through good times and bad, in light and in darkness. The building is a living reminder of our need to recognise the tradition from which we come and to embrace 'the changes and chances of this fleeting world'. It is a strange and miraculous survival which enshrines an eternal vision of Christ and his Church that reaches towards the future. Such visitors may arrive as casual holidaymakers or unenthusiastic students, but they leave as pilgrims.

Tom Fleming has used a rough, textured water-colour paper so that some of the letters for this Prayer have a slightly 'broken' effect. The various different colours have been used to create a pattern within the letters.

MAY ALL WHO COME
TO THIS PLACE
AS

VISITORS

FIND HERE

THE PRESENCE

AND

LOVE OF GOD

MAY THEY LEAVE HERE
AS

PILGRIMS

This text was commissioned by a Welshman, Griff Thomas, a historian from Devon with a deep love of Wales and all things Celtic. He was visiting Escomb for the weekend and saw a link between the sacred history of the Northumbrian Saints and the emergence of the Arthurian legends. Both were preserved by monastic scribes. Both tell of a 'Golden Age', a vanished past, and both gave rise to traditions and stories that helped preserve the culture and dignity of people who had been defeated and marginalised.

Arthur has died and Sir Lancelot is remembering words that King Arthur had spoken to him as they were walking through an orchard, dreaming of the future glory of the recently formed fellowship of the Round Table. Arthur's words foreshadow the destruction that is to come, but also contain the reassurance that the sheer power and vision of their deeds will be remembered for all eternity. The Welsh word 'Afallon' (Avalon) translates as 'the land of apples' and is an image of heaven. In the ancient churchyard at Escomb there is a fading Welsh inscription upon one of the grave stones which translates, "And the trumpet shall sound, and the dead shall be raised. The doors to the world's graves on one word will open."

A reputed site for Lancelot's castle is at Bamburgh in Northumberland, close to Lindisfarne.

Susan Moor who illuminated the text is an experienced Scribe and tutor for the group.

we will make
such a blaze
that men will
REMEMBER US
upon the
OTHER SIDE
of the
DARK.

In giving his permission to use this text, Bishop Kallistos Ware, a leading member of the Greek Orthodox tradition in the British isles, writes,

'"Acquire inner peace, and thousands around you will find their salvation", said the Russian 19th century teacher St. Seraphim of Sarov. If we learn to wait in stillness upon God, even for just a few minutes each day, this will give unity and depth to all other things we do. We shall be available to others, open and compassionate, in a way that would not otherwise be possible. Our actions will become a source of healing and our words will become words of fire.

I remember with pleasure my visits to your beautiful church. May God bless the Book of Escomb.'

Conditions for the calligraphers in the church were extremely cold despite the use of a number of heaters, and a warm fire in the Saxon Inn over the road. The discipline needed to fight off the chill was a factor in the execution of this text. The lettering is in a modern uncial.

UNLESS

THERE IS A CENTRE IN THE MIDDLE OF A STORM, UNLESS A MAN IN THE MIDST OF ALL HIS ACTIVITIES, PRESERVES A SECRET ROOM IN HIS HEART, WHERE HE STANDS ALONE BEFORE GOD, THEN HE WILL LOSE ALL SENSE OF SPIRITUAL DIRECTION AND BE TORN TO PIECES.

KALLISTOS WARE 'SILENCE IN PRAYER'
Jim Pollard

A THEME PRAYER

ominic James was commissioned to illuminate this ancient Gaelic prayer which is used as a theme prayer by the congregation at Escomb. The Church is known as 'the Saxon church', but the feel of the place with its circular churchyard and origins lost in the mists of time is as much Celtic as it is Saxon. In our relationship with God there is always mystery. We do not know all the answers and there are times when we cannot see clearly, but if we can hold His hand and feel His presence in the darkness, it is enough.

The script used for this prayer text is uncial.

A Gaelic Prayer

"As the rain hides the stars,
as the autumn mist
hides the hills,
As the clouds veil
the blue of the sky
so the dark happenings
of my lot hide
the shining of thy face
from me.

Yet if I may hold
thy hand in the darkness
it is enough.......
since I know, that
though I may stumble
in my going
thou dost not fall."

a small flame

This is an ancient Celtic prayer which pictures the life of the believer as a small flame, kindled by the spirit of Christ. The decoration serves to reinforce the relationship between 'Spirit' and 'Light' in God's revelation of himself through the faith of the believer in this dark and uncertain world.

The theme of this prayer is reflected in the prayer of dismissal used after every service in the Saxon church:

"May the light of Christ continue to shine among us in this place. And may we bear true and faithful witness to that light. Amen".

Susan Doel has produced this text in a modernised half-uncial hand, with letters and knotwork derived from the style used in the Lindisfarne Gospels.

KINDLE·THIS
LITTLE·LIGHT

kindle this little light
on the earthly plane.
I dedicate it to the service
of the Spirit.
I guard and cherish this
light as a living symbol,
and an act of faith in
the reality of the promise
of Light.

THE UNDERLYING VISION

This prayer was handed to Dominic James by one of the congregation at Escomb. Every church should be a home, and every Christian home should be an image of God's Kingdom, where He is the centre and focus of all family life. This theme relates to the underlying vision of Escomb where "the people, pastor and place shall be one in the service of Christ" (p.31).

Lord God,

our heavenly Father,

we pray you to

bless this house

that it may be a place of

peace, safety

and comfort

⁜

give grace to all

who enter in

that they may

do so to your

praise & glory

for the sake of

Jesus christ

our lord,

amen.

GOD AND HIS CREATION

The 'knotwork' which provides the base of this text from Psalm 118 was created by using a variegated water colour wash outlined in opaque gouache. The knotwork and use of animals for illustration stresses one of the great themes of Celtic and Northumbrian illumination, that of the inter-connectedness of God and his creation. Humans achieve worth and dignity through their relationship to God, with each other and their reverence and respect for their fellow creatures.

The text is written in uncial by Freda Miller,
and the initial letter is in the Celtic 'zoomorphic' style
which uses animals or birds as a motif.

This is the day the Lord has made. We will rejoice and be glad in it.

psalm 118·24

INNOCENT SUFFERING

This text is from Bede's hymn for the Feast of the Holy Innocents (December 28th). The murder of the children in Bethlehem, ordered by King Herod after the birth of Jesus, is a witness to the redemption of evil through the innocent suffering of Jesus on the Cross.

The Venerable Bede lived from 673-735 a.d. and spent virtually all his life in the joint monastery of Jarrow-Monkwearmouth. His work is one of the most important sources for the understanding of early English History. Although he lived at the same time as the building of the church at Escomb, there is no direct reference to Escomb in his writings. His remains were taken from the monastery in Jarrow by Elfrid Westou in the early to mid 11th century, and are now interred in the Galilee Chapel in Durham Cathedral (see the dedication on p.27).

Uncials have been used for the main Latin text.
In the tradition of the Lindisfarne Gospels Donald Tate has written
the English translation using a smaller, less formal hand
in the form of a 'gloss' between the lines of the larger script.
The decorations are in the style of Celtic knotwork.

Hymnum canentes martyrum

chanting a hymn of joyous praise

Dicamus innocentium

we sing martyrs who are innocent,

Quos terra flendo perdidit

whom the earth relinquished in tears,

Gaudens sed aethra suscipit

whom the heavens receive rejoicing.

Uultum patris per saecula

whose face the angels of the lord

Quorum tuentur angeli

gaze on in peace forever,

Eiusque laudant gratium

and praise his mercy

Hymnum canentes martyrum

chanting a hymn of joyous praise.

DEAR LORD AND FATHER

Ray Wilson has produced this text in an insular half-uncial script with a Celtic cross and a border of knotwork. This style is characteristic of Britain from the 7th to the 9th centuries and is called 'insular' because of its connection with the British Isles, including Ireland. The verse is drawn from the popular hymn "Dear Lord and Father of mankind" by J.G. Whittier (1807-92).

The Cross is the focus and the text breaks through the knotwork preventing a purely enclosed and self-sufficient understanding of faith.

DROP thy still dews of quietness

till all our strivings cease

take from our souls the strain and stress

and let our ordered lives confess

the beauty of thy peace

R.WILSON. APRIL '95.

DELIBERATE AMBIGUITY

This Dedication is by the scholar Alcuin of York (735-804). Alcuin was born in Northumbria in 735 a.d., the same year in which Bede died. He was educated at York under Archbishop Egbert, a distinguished pupil of Bede, and Ethelbert the Master of the school there who succeeded as Archbishop in 767 a.d.. He was later invited to the Frankish court by Charlemagne who became his patron. Alcuin was instrumental in the renaissance of culture and learning that spread throughout the Frankish Empire and Europe.

He wrote a number of important religious biographies, and letters complaining about the falling standards of personal behaviour in England. It seems that such criticism has persisted over the past 1200 years.

The text is written in uncials by Freda Miller.
A Celtic cross in knotwork has been used for decoration.
There is a deliberate ambiguity where the word in the script which looks like 'Life', is pronounced in modern English as "live".

DEDICATION

BE AN honour to the church,
   follow christ's word,
clear in thy task and
   careful in thy speech,
be thine an open hand,
   a merry heart,
christ in thy mouth, life
   that all men may know
a lover of righteousness
   and compassion.
let none come to thee
   and go sad away.

ALCUIN OF YORK
735-804 FM

The Light of Life

This transcription by Anne Mawson is from the memorial to Dean and Mrs. Cyril Alington on the wall above the tomb of the Venerable Bede in the Galilee Chapel at the West end of Durham Cathedral. The text is a translation by Sir Roger Mynors, formerly Professor of Latin at Oxford and Dean Alington's son-in-law, of words by Bede. The words are from Bede's Commentary on the Book of Revelation, and have been reproduced with the kind permission of the Dean and Chapter of Durham. There is the contrast in ideas between "the night of this world is past" and "the light of life, and opens everlasting day".

The capitals are derived by Anne from various medieval manuscripts.
The small letters are uncials, based on the script used at
the joint monastery of Wearmouth-Jarrow,
by the monks at the home of Bede.

CHRIST *

is the

MORNING

STAR *

who, when

the night of this world is past

brings to his saints

the promise of

the light of life,

and opens

EVERLASTING

DAY

VENERABLE BEDE   ANNE MAWSON

INSPIRATION

This anonymous verse was found inscribed on the fly-leaf of an old Bible. Jim Pollard sees it as giving expression to the inspiration and vocation which underlies his work as a Scribe.

The capitals are in water colour outlined in ink
and the lettering is in uncial.

Could we with ink the ocean fill,
Were every stalk on earth a quill,
And were the skies of parchment made,
And every man a scribe by trade,
To tell the love of God alone,
Would drain the ocean dry,
Nor could a scroll, contain the whole,
Though stretched from sky to sky.

ANONYMOUS VERSE ON FLY-LEAF OF AN OLD BIBLE
Jim Pollard

SERMONS IN STONE

This text encapsulates the vision of the church at Escomb. It is developed from one of the themes of the film Excalibur which tells the story of King Arthur. In the quest for the Holy Grail which will revitalise the kingdom and counter the destruction of Mordred and the moral decay expressed in the relationship of Lancelot and Guinevere, the secret of the Grail is described as "The King and the land are one". So we understand that in the life of the Church at Escomb, the people, the pastor and the place should be one, and that the holiness of the place is to be found as much in its people as in its past. The focus of all sacred history, worship and ministry is to be found in the service of the living Christ. Ancient churches have been described as 'sermons in stone', but without people to pray and care, they become dead ruins.

Tom Fleming has used italic script and capitals of two different weights to create differences of emphasis in the various parts of the text. There is a deliberate intermingling of concepts and colours.

The
People
Pastor
place

SHALL·BE·AS·ONE
in the service of

·C·H·R·I·S·T

Tom Fleming

COMFORTABLE WORDS

This text forms the introduction and initial Biblical verse used in "the comfortable words" found in the 1662 Book of Common Prayer Service of Holy Communion.

Douglas Fairbairn brings out the difference in mood between the optimism and activity of the introduction and the weariness of the believer seeking refreshment in the verse from St. Matthew's Gospel 11, 28.

The two parts of the text have been written in contrasting styles and colours. The first part is based on an English Caroline minuscule and the second part is an insular half-uncial, the script used for the Lindisfarne Gospels.

Hear what comfortable words our Saviour Christ saith unto all that truly turn to him.

Come unto me all ye that labour and are heavy laden and I will give you rest.

MATTHEW XI : 28

Doug. Fairbairn
3/95

THE INNOCENT CHILDREN

his is a continuation of Bede's hymn for the Feast of the Holy
Innocents on p.19. The cruel suffering of the innocent children on
earth at the hands of King Herod is contrasted with the warmth and
love of their welcome in heaven.

*Uncials have been used for the main Latin text, and the
English translation has been written in a smaller less formal hand
in the form of a "gloss".*

QUOS REX PEREMIT IMPIUS

those whom the wicked king destroyed,

PIUS SED AUCTOR COLLIGIT

the merciful creator now receives

SECUM BEATOS COLLOCANS

in the light of the perpetual realm,

IN LUCE REGNI PERPETIS

drawing to himself the blessed ones.

QUI MANSIONES SINGULIS

he who grants mansions to all

LARGITUS IN DOMO PATRIS

inside his father's house,

DONAT SUPERNIS SEDIBUS

now grants eternal dwelling-place

QUOS REX PEREMIT IMPIUS

to those whom the wicked king destroys.

A LIGHT IN THE WORLD

ere we see an illustration of the first part of a well-known Methodist children's hymn:

"Jesus bids us shine with a pure clear light, like a little candle burning in the night". (Susan Warner 1819-85)

The written text only includes the first line of the verse, but the words have been shaped into a candle and the flame contrasts red and orange against the black of the night. This type of illustration is called a calligram where the words are arranged so that they make a shape related to the text.

The letters are written with the pen held at a fairly flat angle. The resulting effect is one of innocence and purity, appropriate for a baby brought to baptism where the family are given a lighted candle so that the newly baptised child may "shine as a light in the world to the glory of God the Father".

The scribe Janet Barnett felt that the text required a very open interpretation of uncial. Note the characteristic wedge-shaped lead-in strokes (serifs).

jesus
bids
us
SHINE
with
* a *
pure
clear
light

a "gift" in the making

Again this prayer is written in the form of a calligram, where the words are arranged so that they make a shape related to the text. The composer of the Chalice Prayer was Frances Nuttall. She was a craft member of the Society of Scribes and Illuminators. The Rev'd Robert Cooper of the Arts and Recreation Chaplaincy in the North East tells of a conversation with her where she said that the words and design of the prayer came to her as a "gift" in the making of the Work. She died in 1983 aged 91.

In the offering of the cup at the Eucharist, we seek to be filled with the light, love and life of Christ so that we may be a container which overflows with his grace to all with whom we come into contact. There are echoes of the words of St. Paul in his Second letter to the Corinthians, "We have this treasure in earthen vessels, to show that the transcendent power belongs to God and not to us" (Ch.4.7).

Doreen Simm has used an uncial script and a surround of red ink to highlight the shape of the chalice.

The Prayer of the Chalice

Father to thee I raise my whole being
a vessel emptied of self. accept lord
this my emptiness and so fill me
with thy self. thy light, thy love,
thy life, that these thy precious
gifts may radiate through me
and overflow the chalice of
my heart into the hearts
of all with whom I come
in contact this week
revealing unto
them
the
Beauty of thy joy
and
the
serenity
of thy peace
which nothing can destroy

GOODNESS IS MULTI-COLOURED

The text is from St. Paul's letter to the Romans, Ch.12, 9. Tom Fleming uses an italic script and a variety of water colours which have been allowed to run into one another. The use of red for "Hate what is evil" is particularly striking. Love and goodness are multi-coloured and gentle, hatred is shown as single-minded and passionate.

Let LOVE be genuine,

HATE what is evil

HOLD FAST to what is GOOD

Romans 12 v 9

Tom Fleming

TEMPTATION

This poem was created and written down by Dominic James, one of the Northumbrian Scribes. It is based on the theme of the Roman Catholic Mass readings for the 5th of March, 1995 (First Sunday in Lent) the weekend when the Scribes came to visit Escomb. The theme in most Church traditions for this Sunday is the temptation of Christ in the wilderness, and the underlying Biblical texts are Deuteronomy, Ch.26, 4-10 and Luke Ch.4, 1-13. We too must follow Christ into the wilderness to face our own Satanic voices.

Our way lies through the wilderness
Lord, our needs we now confess,
spirit fill us, Jesus bless,
Father, hear your children.

heavy with our tiredness
tempted towards sinfulness,
spirit fill us, Jesus bless,
Father, hear your children.

lost, despairing, in distress,
seeing nought but emptiness,
spirit fill us, Jesus bless,
Father hear your children.

filled with our own mightiness
straying from your gentleness
spirit fill us, Jesus bless,
Father, hear your children.

in the depths of worldly darkness
grant us your eternal brightness.
spirit fill us, Jesus bless us,
Father, hear your children.

dominic james.

A FRANCISCAN BLESSING

This text is based on the opening verse of Psalm 67 and is used as a prayer of Blessing by Franciscans, as these were the words used by St. Francis when he blessed his disciple Brother Leo. The illustration is drawn in water colour where the soft shades of the colours harmonise with the warmth and light of the prayer for God's blessing and protection.

Jim Pollard has written the blessing in the form of an English Caroline minuscule.

the LORD

bless us and keep us,
the LORD make his
face to shine upon us,
and be gracious unto
us, the LORD lift up
the light of his
countenance upon
us and give us peace.

"BASED ON THE OPENING VERSE OF PSALM 67"

Jim Pollard

seek simplicity and sincerity

These verses are from the Sermon on the Mount from St. Matthew's Gospel Ch.5, 5, 8. They have been written in modernised insular half-uncial by Susan Moor. Scribes are, by calling, traditionalists in that their task has been to pass on the wisdom of the past to future generations. However, the really great scribes have also been innovators both in terms of the originality of their designs and also through their compiling and editing of texts. The verses are important for those who are drawn to Escomb and who would respond to the enduring appeal of Northumbrian spirituality.

The great Norman cathedral at Durham is magnificent in its size and architecture and is justly recognised as one of the finest buildings in the world. The Saxon church at Escomb is a complete contrast in its smallness and simplicity. It is a church for little people and for those who are drawn to hidden places. There are no great saints known to have been associated with the building of the church. The people of Escomb were for many centuries servants to the Prince Bishops of Durham at Auckland Castle. Later, they worked in the mines and forged the first railway tracks of iron. The neighbouring village of Witton Park was the original terminus of the Stockton and Darlington Railway, but few outside the two villages remember that brief moment of glory. We have learnt how to survive in times of change and upheaval. We know that after the despoilment and destruction of slag heaps and coal mines, the grass will grow, and we can reclaim the land. We have faith that if we seek simplicity and sincerity then we shall find God amid "the changes and chances of this fleeting world."

Susan Moor has written these two Beatitudes in a modern half-uncial using contemporary design work for her illumination, while at the same time preserving a recognisable continuity with the work of the monastic scribes of Lindisfarne and Jarrow-Monkwearmouth.

blessed

are the meek:
for they shall inherit
the earth.

blessed

are the pure in heart:
for they shall see God.

matthew, chapter 5

acknowledgements

The Rev'd Robert Cooper, Chaplain to the Arts and Recreation in the North East, for guidance on the calligraphy.

Mr. Roger Norris, Deputy Librarian of The Dean and Chapter Library at Durham Cathedral, for guidance on the historical references.

Mrs. Wendy Robertson, Mrs. Elsie Kitching, Mrs. Anne Manners, Mrs. Elizabeth Taylor and Mrs. Elizabeth Jones for their support and advice with the editing and presentation.

S.P.C.K. (Society for Promoting Christian Knowledge) and S.T.L. (Send The Light) for their help with marketing.

Pindar plc and AdverSet Design & Reprographics for their guidance on layout and setting.

Wear Valley District Council and Durham County Council for their support, and assistance with publication and promotion.

Any mistakes are the responsibility of Nicholas Beddow.

WEAR
VALLEY
DISTRICT COUNCIL

County
Durham

Land of the Prince Bishops